IRIADA TALES

Iriada Tales

poetry collection

BY IRENE SMIRNOVA

Atelier Bloom Editions

Copyright © 2024 by by Irene Smirnova

All rights reserved. No part of this book may be reproduced in any manner whatsoever without written permission except in the case of brief quotations embodied in critical articles and reviews.

First Printing, 2024

Dedicated to my Family.

Thank you to my daughters Eulita and Sonia, my son-in-law Arturs and my dearest husband Alexis to encourage my writing and inspiring me through out my life. Thank you to my friends, whose words of wisdom and humour always resonate as encouragement and critique.
Special thank you to Aparna Kumar, whose edit helped me to view my poetry from an other perspective.
I write poetry and make art all my life, sharing it with a world is a privilege and a delight. Hope you be able to see the world as I do through the kaleidoscope of these poems. Hope they will bring you joy.

1
NATURE

~ 1 ~

CLIMB THE TREE

And climb the tree to write some words
And listen to the singing birds
And count the clouds shades on grass
And wave to boats as they pass
Be drunk with freedom of the air
With no time to waste and spare
And as we climb the trees of life
Stay young in our wild hearts
The sun is rising in the sky
The water in the glass is dry
Yet no one listens to the time
And keeps on climbing till they die

June 2024

~ 2 ~

WHITE NIGHT

Don't call out white night,
She is still blind and meek.
Don't wake up city lights,
Let them blink and sleep.

Without answers, streetlights,
Without familiar doors.
Night will write its trace,
Stay as a milky fog.

Moonlight
Crawling on the broken wall.
The night smears the day,
The day smears the night,
Where colours are blurred and bleak.

It will sound as a forgotten verse.
Resemble a garden fresco,
Slowly fading and leaves
Dropping transparent petals
On grungy mosaic floor.

Just as the darkness devoured
My city and all the above,
I heard someone else calling it
Endless, resembling a still life
Night.

November 2000

~ 3 ~

THEY CALL YOU SNOW

The shapes of trees are not like I remembered
From yesterday.
The slopes are covered with the icy dust
From strange cold...

The looping cold derails thoughtsg
And vintage smell
Fills all the gaps in windows where wind
Can sneak in.

The shapes of trees are all covered with
New snow,
New way of colouring the time,
The seasons change,

The lovely change of soul,
Whose tears running
Turn into the ice.
The shapes of drapes are covered all with snow.

Abandoned house
Just as we remembered it in the past;

And yet it is renewed and blooming
With snow brush.

With swooshing snow brush...

January 2024

~ 4 ~

LULLABY

I feel like I am the mother of the earth
And lullaby is well due.
With the soothing motion of my voice
That echoes deep in the universe.
And echo teaches me to love
To keep it as a song.

December 2023

~ 5 ~

MARCH WALK

We walk tiny steps
Along spring,
Follow the brook singing,
Pretending to be an ocean.

We move against wooly air,
Tickling us with March frost
Against our foggy breath,
Our words, our thoughts.

But all this spring nonsense
Suddenly becomes
A balloon of inspiration,
Popping just in time
And sparkle with a steam.

Ecstatic, joyful, fast
Inviting steps for imagination.
What happens to the drops
Once in a steam they reach the ocean?

Those frosty tears of mine

Were carried by the wind
And reached the stream
With dreamy grass
With shimmery sand.

March 2024

~ 6 ~

AUTUMN EYES

I hear whisper of the leaves
Following every step
Voices of the yellow trees
Breathing the air of fall.
Holding my breath in fear
Of cold winter days ahead.
Swiping the leaves to piles
To dive in the piles with joy.
Childish jumps in puddles,
Blunt jokes about the rain,
Conversations starters
Around cold winter day.
Yet whispers of leaves are haunting
Rumours, revolts, mistrust.
All in one day of autumn
Yellow doesn't last.

July 2023

~ 7 ~

PATERNS

I draw a circle
And arrange the flowers,
Like daisies in a strange and unpredictable fashion.
Like blue clouds in a place of whites.
Drops of tears
Of the coloured rain.
I arrange them in wired shapes
And patterns,
So, they make illusions of an orderly state.
The enigmatic order,
That is artificial,
Man made. Is there logic
Or just an intuitive movement,
That brings together
A state of things?

July 2023

~ 8 ~

A SEASON OF DUST

Behind the sheen of leaves,
Turned blue in the sun
Drops that are near...
I hear them singing
The song of grey dust.
Of dreams, diving deep...
Of floating emotions...
The season of dust
Almost gone.

June 2022

~ 9 ~

MOON

The crescent moon dipped in the darkness of Chocolate night
And sprinkled with sugary stars.
A bitter taste of August -
Best Dessert of Paris,
Blueberry blues of cloudy Montmartre.
Hush brown bears of Turilles gardens fair.
Citronelle grass, mint orange ice-cream and
Lemon tarts.
Always sprinkle some laughter
As a final touch.

June 2022

~ 10 ~

GHOSTS

Drifting ghosts of unfinished thoughts
That wash the roofs at night and dawn,
They sail this city ship with wind
To reach unknown shores of dreams.
They make the roads for us to see
In thin air of city seams,
Appearing for us with fog.
Some see it as a simple smog.
There are some swishing sounds they make
That sing to you to stay awake.
Although you thirsty in your sleep
And so unsure when you step.
The city words in simple trash
To fly away, to stay free.

October 2023

~ 11 ~

FOUR SEASONS

The whispers call me from depth of the ocean
To tell the story of the seasons change.
Green brush outlines
The contour of each tree,
The golden aura sunlit,
They call it fall
For the reason
Of change.
I call it a wise season,
When losing the foliage,
You gain the patience
And silence
In front of the different life,
That lasts there for four long months.
Monochrome life,
With every snowflake differ only in sunlight
By nuance
In colour,
But shades of white
Reflecting.
Monochrome as a backdrop
For small reflections

Of sunshine,
As a colour brush.
They call it winter.
To be true, the snow
Covers all the surfaces.
And it is crisp,
Thin,
Untouchable sometimes...
We call it fragile.
Sun plays with it
And days,
Some days
It sounds
With few breaks,
Few cracks,
Few drips.
It makes sound waves
That resonate through all the surfaces.
And winter sings.
And when that happens
The colours break the ice.
And so, it starts with song
Bell of waterfall,
The stream,
The fountain,
The rivers
And the lakes.
They move the ice
With shimmer,
Tremble,
Fever.
They colour ice with sun
That runs its brush
With faster blurred broad strokes.

And so, goes spring
From monochrome to colour
In one blurred bloom
Of petals blooms and buds,
Poking through the ice
With sound of music
To free the colour
From the winter dream.
They call it spring fever
When this music echoes
In the hearts of lovers.
And then spills into the stream
Called summer.
Heated,
Foggy,
Summer, full of love.
We call it full bloom,
Lush greens,
Dusty sand,
Squashing heat,
Drenching thirst,
Stormy waves.
All kind of weathered
Emotions
Summer can bring.
And then it decays into fall.

September 2023

~ 12 ~

LILY

Water lily, oh lily,
I have found your dreams
In deep ocean waters
Were lilies won't dare
Reaching these floors...
They tangle me softly
And bring back the songs
That sailors were singing
That seagulls forgot...

March 2024

~ 13 ~

UNTITLED

Shimmering story of river
Spilling waters like crazy
Spring bound,
Spring tamed.
Spring calling
Only if you are listening,
Only if you are.
It is calling me,
This river,
Just takes me with it.
Losing my canoe
Just on my way to see you,
So, I will swim.
I will be there at your steps
Signing this song with river
Ringing all bells of spring
Playing my guitar
Till breaking all the strings.

December 2023

~ 14 ~

PUDDLES

Walking on puddles, jumping,
Smashing glass ice on the edges,
Catching the falling snowflakes,
Falling in wings of an angel
Who hides under the snow.
Some would forget the ecstatic
Feeling of childish decisions,
When it comes to the snow
Falling on branches of oak,
Leaving dunes on its path on the ground.

August 2023

~ 15 ~

MOON DANCE

I am sleeping on a bridge
That moon has drawn for us
Across the ocean sky,
Across the universe.
Where we have danced alone
And left the sparkly trace,
After the moon dance glow,
After the sun broke the rays,
Against the clouds' row…

July 2023

~ 16 ~

DESERT

Dreaming with desert about colours of green
With mint and sage,
Some mixed with blue.
And only you
Could have seen
Clouds listening to our secret.
Dreaming with ice about shades of blue
With turquoise and indigo,
Mixing the edges,
Swirling on canvas,
Making a template to print.
Dreaming with snow about the colours,
All shades in rainbow mix,
Sparkling with rays of sun,
Dripping in spring,
Winking with crystal blink.

June 2023

~ 17 ~

CLOUDS

Do clouds mock me
With birds fly
Nearby
When wind is laughing
Brushing
Hair
Like a bird nest.
Does the sun have serious
Intentions
When freckling
My nose
And my cheeks?

June 2023

~ 18 ~

ROSES DON'T CRY

I don't see roses cry
When dry leaves drop dust to the ground.
They know seasons change,
And sun returns with rain
To carry them around.

March 2024

~ 19 ~

PULSE OF ANCESTRY

We are a bunch of heartbeats,
Pulses of ancestry.
We are pulsars of the universe
And stars in someone's sky.

January 2024

~ 20 ~

LEAVES ARE FALLING

The leaves are falling,
The years are falling
Behind me and behind you.
Temperature rising
In our emotions
Behind the curtain,
Behind the doors.
Arguments thrown,
Attitudes swollen.
Bridges are burnt
Borders are shut.
Nevertheless
We continue to lie,
Strangers on planet
Ready to die.
Nevertheless
Someone there is born,
Blossoming, flourishing,
Ready for change.

August 2023

~ 21 ~

FISHING

Come fish for the stars with me
And make the nets with grass.
The stars are hypnotic
And catch us in nets
As souls that in love
Are easily trapped.
I am waiting for a kiss
On glowing moon road
Somewhere in middle
Of deep purple lake.
I cross then the path
Swim towards the horizon
To splash them with stars
In the same fishing net.
Come with me fishing...

August 2023

~ 22 ~

BREATHING SOUND

When you breathe air
That is pulsating with the sound,
Do you breathe a sound?

Do you feel the waves
Of its guitar
Or sirens of the ambulance,
Rushing through traffic
Or a pile of rubbish
Flying from a scratching sound,
Of garbage truck door opening?

Do you hear whispers
And breathe them?
Like thoughts of trembling leaves
That wave to you
When you feel all these sounds.

Do you breathe them,
Their pulsating waves
Resonating in your blood vessels
Oxygen filled and pulsating

With each wave of sound
With each vibration.

March 2024

2

FABLES

~ 23 ~

A MAN WITH A PILE OF LETTERS

Steep road would be small for his ambition,
He would choose a mountain instead
To carry rocks and carve the letters
Out of them,
Throw them off the cliff
On the other side.
The letters formed a mountain of sort
And that became a way for him to live,
Make letters out of rocks,
Make mountains of them.
They do not form
By any means
The words,
Just pile of letters—
Simple, shaped,
Without form
That brings them to the purpose.
He knew one thing—
To form a word
He would destroy the mountain of letters
And all his letters would be crushed,
All mountains would parish.

He chose to walk a road that steep,
Come to the ground, carve the letters
And form a word,
That would make sense,
That would mean purpose.

August 2023

A LENS OF TIME

When we are born,
A blank paper list
In front of us
Will be unfolded.
We are loved,
Till things evolve
Though lens of time.
Would you consider human nature change?
Would you evolve with time
Or skip the lesson?
Would you ask for more?
Would you regret
Being who you are
In lens of time?
It ties us to the common earth,
But brings us to the different house,
Space differs
In the lens of time.
Blank paper
Suddenly is filled with doodles,
That scratch the naiveté
And filled with colours.

Where someone draws the borders
Of existence,
Like cage
Around choices
In the sense of time.
We reach the grave
With paperless emotions,
As no space is left
In our book of life.
But there is one page
Left blank,
Referrals.
We won't read it,
It is reserved for time.

July 2023

~ 25 ~

IF I WOULD BECOME A NIGHT

If I would become a night,
I would look for chestnut shades,
So deep and so dark.
If I would become a cloud,
Reaching for passages in sky
Between the mountains of troubles,
I would cry with a rain,
Drench in its crazy freshness,
Cold and enlightening.
That would turn all these emotions
Upside down, so people
Would abandon their umbrellas,
Just to stay with the rain,
Just to become a rain,
To return to their senses.

October 2023

~ 26 ~

PURPOSE OF LIFE

"What is the purpose of life?"
She said.
"What is life",
He answered her softly.
"There is no purpose,
There is only life,
With the extraordinary and common,
Indifferent and engaged."
Somewhere she believed him,
But decided to dig further.
Years passed as she searched for purpose,
For the meaning of being there
For her, for him, for little ones, for other people,
For everyone indeed.
She felt engaged, as he described it,
Discovered everything fantastic and unique,
She coloured life in her own colours,
And found books that speak.
She made her space like any other artist.
She made some friends and enemies along.
And what about the purpose?
It was discovered once on her way home.

She saw a man holding a flower
And giving it to a homeless man.
Another smiled, gave it back and whispered,
"God bless and give it to your friend."
We share thoughts, discover worlds and beauty
And being capable to create.
The purpose is to live creating
and giving beauty back.
She met him in a restaurant in Soho
And told him proudly,
"I found a purpose man!"
He smiled at her,
Then hugged and gave her a flower.
A flower he received from a homeless man.

July 2023

~ 27 ~

RAIN SONG

There was a sound with a rain,
That played a song with wind along:
"Don't be a shadow
Of your desire and your greed,
Don't be an indicator of a wind.
Be a wind, be a storm, a torrential rain
To run your life in sweat and pain.
Because the sweeter the reward,
Because the shadows fade and vanish,
Because the indicators tarnish.
But impact stays
With long-lasting sun rays.
But just remember one drop
Will not make you a waterfall."

August 2023

~ 28 ~

THEY LIED

Lie, they told me. Lie.
Walk on the burning rocks,
Lie how it feels.
Act like no one is watching,
Feel like everyone does.
Speak like no one will listen,
Talk like reverb will pulse.
Live like you hear through walls,
Act like words will pass.
Jump on thin ice like feather,
Touch shiny velvet like steel,
Drink river of daily water
Like hours of endless surprise.

October 2023

~ 29 ~

ELABORATE

There is potential
To make the world
A more complex place,
Elaborate,
Carved from marble,
With lots of details
That marvel us with skills
And
Attention to meticulous detail.
Unprecedented,
Unique,
Breathtaking beauty
Of elaborate work
Of a talented person,
Who shared his skill,
Put his meaning to timely effort.
There is also a way
To make a plane simple world
With repetitive structures
And call it essential.
Call it minimal,
Pure.

The world with no skills,
No knowledge acquired,
No margin of error
When the straight line is cut.
The world of simple
Is easy to learn,
And forget,
Reproduce,
Replicate.
What is your world
You admire,
Cherish,
Carry on,
Pass along?

January 2024

~ 30 ~

METAMORPHOSIS

Shapeless time is the only thing,
that cannot take form of another,
it holds all shapes within.

January 2024

~ 31 ~

TRAVELLERS

Bewildered traveler lost in a desert once
Has stumbled upon a rounded rock.
Winds carved it, smoothed the surface,
It looked like alien ship from the far.
He thought it might be carved for him to sit
Under the burning sun and meditate.
And leaned upon a turtle's back
Until it moved away like alien ship…
We stumble upon different things
That make us wonder of our purpose
That transforms in time,
Carved by the wind of change and others…
We are all bewildered by the change, shocked,
As a rigid mind is used to seeing things
In a familiar and common order.
We are all travelers discovering the rock…

April 2024

~ 32 ~

MEDITATE

A touch of ice, freezing emotions,
Brining closer to still life.
Burning sensation on cheeks and lips,
Bubbling sensation when breathing,
Brushing with cold air snowflakes
On my lashes.
Meditative landscape of winter.

March 2024

~ 33 ~

BLUE ROOM

You were singing a song
About a blue room.
I imagined peacocks
And colourful skies.
I imagined a woman
In deep red dress,
Walking towards me and smiling
Wondering smile,
Strangely enough
She was welcoming,
Warm and inviting
With her deep red colour.
I remember nothing,
Except the smell of her red velvet dress
And the curtain,
Deep blue curtain.
The magic or dance
And the song that you sang,
Deleted the memory,
It might be a part of seduction.
But since then, I see
Blue rooms like this,

With a woman in red,
Her lips are still smiling.

December 2010

~ 34 ~

AND THE SUN GOT CAUGHT IN A FERRIS WHEEL

And the sun got caught in a Ferris wheel
And the man got trapped in ambitions self.
No shame, no waste, no curse, no will.
No road is straight to the top of hill.
Sun has spilled its rays on Champs Élysées,
Turned table fast towards, betrayed and left.
Man, who seen success has become obsessed
With the rays of dust that transcend from stars.
But the stars got caught in the Ferris wheel
And desires rise and ambition fade.
As the crescent moon draws the narrow bridge,
Steps are fast and meek on the other end.
And the sun got caught in a Ferris wheel…

August 2021

~ 35 ~

CROSSROADS

I saw an architect who,
Standing on the crossroads,
Was shattering his dreams
Against upcoming traffic.
He couldn't make a decision on the spot,
Make up his mind.
And so, he told a lie
For those
Who were impatiently waiting for his answer.
The lie then would come back
To haunt him with the sound
Of honking cars, of scrunching sound of trains.
Of the beeping noise of garbage trucks and pickups.
There was no room for cardinals to sing.
Crossroads fade in distant past,
We recognize them only from a distance.
They don't appear as a crossroad first
As other path is drawn for us sometimes
In a perspective of reflecting time.
This man was just an architect
Whose dreams made pattern
For the city plan.

He didn't think of self
As much importance person,
But life proofread
His dreamy thoughts
And found spelling errors.
Too late to interfere
As his dreams made their way
And coloured grey
The asphalt, trees and windows,
Erasing the reflections joy.

March 2024

~ 36 ~

MOVIE ON A BRIDGE

I stood behind your shoulder
Filming the outline
Of your figure on dim background
With murky lights.
Deep voice would tremble,
There is someone behind you
Always. I don't see him,
Although I know his voice.
In each dream we move forward
The endless scene of this movie,
With thousands of retakes
That patiently I erase.
And so, it goes again
The desert, the city, the man,
The lights, sound of cars
And voice resembling a scam.
Then suddenly man turns around,
Breaks silence with steps on the ground.
I film the mysterious figure behind
His ego questioned him always.
His double was silent this time,
They looked like twins to me.

My film was about this town
And turned out about this man.
About his ego and questions,
The monologue he switched,
About things we answered
While filming the scene on a bridge.

September 2023

3

DREAMS

~ 37 ~

A WOMAN IN A HONEYCOMB DRESS

I squeezed your hands tight,
Moving towards you.
Your steps are slow and uneven,
Your hands are so cold and weak.
You smell like honey,
Sweet and tender.
The dress is made of honeycomb
And combed by bees
In late September,
When grass is yellow from heat.
They weave the flowers in your hair,
And bend the vines around your neck.
I never feared bees,
Liked honey.
I hold your hand tight,
Woman wrapped in a honeycomb dress.

August 2023

~ 38 ~

GHOSTS OF HORSES

Ghosts of horses were passing through time
Drinking dew when flying.
Time frozen still,
Weakened with wonder.

Sound of horses echoed in the forest
Long after they've gone.
But then there was darkness and smoke
Choking and strangling us
Igniting the trees with thirst.

And horses stamped those fire crackles
And stamped and stamped.
And so, it flows like clouds in the sky
Ghosts of horses
Awaiting invisible goal,
So close to reach.

And sky blended smoothly
With water and foam
Grey-coloured sky
Grey water and bubbles.

With one neutral palette
Water spreader around,
Water travelled around
With herd of invisible horses.

August 2023

~ 39 ~

DEW DREAM

When transparent word becomes a canvas
It reveals the soul.
There was "hello from the outside" this morning,
As if the dawn called me in the sunset.
As if the sunset called me at dawn.
There is a drop of thirst in the dryness of the dream,
But dream has gone; has faded in the fog,
With dew like rain abandoning the day,
And memory erasing joy and all that seems love.

August 2022

~ 39 ~

ILLUSIONS

I would cover my eyes with lace
To see the world in dreams,
To make reality crease
Under pressure perfecting.
Sometimes things aren't as they seem,
Break apart our goals and plans.
But the delicate lace will face
Views that would never change.

March 2024

~ 40 ~

TO DREAM

We dream in deep sleep,
But that is not enough.
We dream in a dream
And see ourselves dreaming.
But that is not enough.
We create artificial world
That shows a dream,
With artificial mind
Drawing a dream
Of us dreaming.
But is that enough?
We stopped dreaming
This way...

September 2020

~ 41 ~

ARTISTIC MIND

River flows, cools downstream,
Our dreams flow
Along the river waves.
We see the works as we imagine
Not as the artist felt it,
As there is a distance,
Enormous distance
Between the images
And feelings as they seem.
Not as material as they are
After all,
Pending our acceptance,
Dreams in the state of a flow.

August 2023

~ 42 ~

PUZZLE

I skipped the word or two,
Created a puzzle
For you to find the clue
Behind a mosaic of senses.
When rain of words
Becomes a music
I want you to sing it,
Live it,
Jump.
Become this rain,
Become a wind,
Become this love,
That weave this puzzle.

August 2021

~ 43 ~

LOOKING FOR OURSELVES

"Do I look so naive", he asked me softly,
I didn't look into his eyes,
Shy and distracted
By the constant presence,
I took a shortcut to his heart.
We charm with those glances,
Brisk movement, play with hair
Falling on the lashes,
A slight nod of the head
Instead of saying "yes".
We were still looking
For tiny ourselves
In others mind.
Not ready to accept
Not ready to retreat.

July 2023

~ 44 ~

UNKNOWN

Home seems far away from the rocky shores of the unknown.
I step on edge and, rushing, run to the horizon.
Where usually the sunshine is spreading rays
And smiles with beaming ways of never-ending hope.
Then usually the falling part appears in a dreamy cloud
And so, we fly above mysterious ground
Above the chasing, screaming, troubled crowd.
The rocky steps are shaped by the troubling worries.
There is always home where someone kind
Will wait for you with arms wide open
With the familiar authentic smile...
So happy landing while the dream is ending...

July 2023

~ 45 ~

WEAKNESS

Sometimes we carry ourselves too much around,
Absorb too much
To change the world
Or so we think.
But too much thirst will wipe us first
So, we forget to water things around.
And as the desert creeps,
Dry wind,
Brisk walks
And little shivers
Of the weakness.
So may be trees that carry leaves
Do that for others.

June 2023

~ 46 ~

A MEDITATIVE PATH

One day you have to take a path
That is unique, that nobody took.
The drift from mainstream,
The shake of the ordinary,
The turn that makes you the one.
It is no easy turn,
You have to shut the doors to the outside,
To stay in silence for a while,
No thoughts, no gestures, no matter.
The state of motionless,
A dream,
Where the path appears
From nowhere by itself.

June 2010

~ 47 ~

CHOICES

Candlelight just melted away
All my dreams.
And some spilled anger
Deep in my veins.
But steps in the darkness
Woke me up again:
"See yourself in reflection of time.
Is it past, is it future
Or present
That you see in reflection?"

May 2022

~ 48 ~

BECOMING WISE

Do not become a trend,
A gig, an entertainment
For those, who
Seek momentum for themselves.
Do not become a dandelion seed
That spreads without purpose,
Directed by the random wind—
Unwanted weed, unroofed soul...
Become a sunshine
Or a rainbow
Or milky stardust
Laughing in the night
For the spontaneous thoughts,
Inspire, nurture.
Be a rock for travelers to lean on,
A path to follow
And a book to read.

May 2022

~ 49 ~

GO WILD

Go wild and run in fields of barley,
Smell tall grass.
Go for tears,
For spreading wings in the air,
Be free, be somewhere fresh.
Don't care about dirt on fingers,
Plant some trees and drink from wells.
Forget the clouds,
Break the patterned fear,
Embrace adventure in your soul.
Enjoy the spark of fireflies at night.
And moonlight, carrying dreams around
And broken laughter of a swallow on a tree.

June 2015

~ 50 ~

AFTER PARTY

Leftovers are cold.
No smoke from cigarettes.
The glass rolling back
To the shelf.
Do you still drink after dark,
Dark memories
Or you confront them
With sugar
Of positive words?

November 2023

~ 51 ~

LIFE IS A WATERFALL

Life is a waterfall—
It never occurred to me.
I feel like a trout in the ocean
With ten feet waves.
Without reflection.
But some value more
The stillness of water,
Reflecting like mirror,
Ignoring the waves,
The motion,
The change.
For me, it's a waterfall,
Timeless,
Evolving,
Crashing the fears
With levelled up game.

January 2024

~ 52 ~

RACING THOUGHTS

When thoughts are racing
                to become some words
We have emotions
                pinching our nerves
But silence resonates
                with a long-lasting hue of blue
To tranquillize them,
                straighten, discipline and structure.
And sentences are usually
                much shorter after that
We steal some standard things
                when we speak.
To be accepted, drain some leftovers
                of the emotional cocktail.
And voice becoming
                softer and so weak...

June 2023

~ 53 ~

EASY PATH

Sometimes the easy path,
The one you take by habit,
Is the longest one.
The one that takes you places
Familiar, in circles.
The path you take
Should only be a part
Of endless journey.
The glimpse of it,
The preview of the quest.
Discover places,
Take in the experience of colours,
Sounds, smells, emotions.
Discover you,
Unknown to yourself.

August 2023

~ 54 ~

BLIZZARD

I want to disappear in the blizzard,
That overwhelming blizzard of my words.
To catch them with my hands, melt down,
To make them water for the thirsty ones.
The stormy clouds of the nasty weather
Will bring emotional and lasted storm,
We need this in a heartless desert
Of drained souls that shine through.

June 2023

~ 55 ~

SUN KISSED

Wake up with sun kissed cheeks,
With a smile softening the expression,
With brave new attitude towards world,
With a thoughtful plan that happens all today.
What if the sun won't kiss your cheeks,
And clouds with smudge the sunshine
With grey monochrome
And fog will blur all plans,
And stormy wind will blow
Thoughts and intentions to be brave.
How would you endure in a world that changes
And bring you challenges
Each second of your breath?
How would you see the change inside
Your soul, that scared soul,
So unable to retreat.

August 2023

~ 56 ~

REBUILDING MYSELF

I am rebuilding myself
From ashes,
I am redrawing myself
From blank.
Without regrets. emotions
No looking back.
I am rethinking the path
No nothing.
Connecting the past
To the future.
I am regretting the debt
To people.
I am rebuilding my soul
From light.

August 2010

~ 57 ~

WORDS BLOSSOM

Before words blossom
Water your emotions,
Melt the fears,
Clear dusty thoughts.
You are not disturbed by things
Surrounding you.
You are disturbed by views
Your take on those things.
They don't impose on you
The judgement or defeat.
The words you choose
Will bounce back,
They have a choice to blossom
Or decay.

November 2023

~ 58 ~

RUNNING AWAY

Running away from still water
In constant emotional drain.
A call of exploring and challenge.
Running away from silence
To hear the voice within.

August 2023

~ 59 ~

CUDDLE IN THE STORM

Touch base with the sound of the soul
To hear waves that beat across the flowing river,
Somewhere between your thoughts and empty mind.
To tame the waves,
To calm them down,
To freeze the river and its sound,
To stay still,
No matter how the waves will flow
Or mind races,
Winds will blow,
You just stay still
In circle with the sunshine
And quite movement slows down with you.
And there it is a void dark space
Of movement in a different pace.
You touch base
With the soul.
Till it sounds deep.

March 2024

~ 60 ~

FROM THE PAST

The voice, echoed heartbeat
And shivering soul
Taking all for granted before.
Suddenly, holding hands with self,
Making peace.
Don't we all have a chance
To be at peace with ourselves?

March 2024

~ 61 ~

RUSHING

Running fast,
Holding breath,
Breaking self,
Taking all,
Giving back.
Don't you cry,
Will stay calm,
Holding brush,
Making art,
Painting over,
Being sober.

January 2024

~ 62 ~

NO RADIO SOUL

You broke the wave,
The frequency,
Turned off reception.
I can't reach you through thick ice.
We were used to raves,
To festivals,
To the crowd waving.
Now, you listen to the empty space.
Adorned, your sleepwalking
In everyday's
Routine and thoughts
Are simple, no ambition left.
I saw this coming
Slowly, with choices
You made along your way.
It didn't matter how it felt.
At least for you,
Turning off
Feelings
One by one
twisted, broken, swept.

December 2023

3

LOVE

~ 63 ~

STITCHED

We stitched together canvas,
Bulletproof in several places,
But later stitches came undone.
No nurse, no doctor, no intervention.

Just you and me together,
All that matters.
Look in my eyes.
I am all yours,
Without smudges and torn apart
Blank papers.

They all have something there to say.
And all that's written here to stay.
Our wounds will heal,
But words will not.

They sting like bees,
And leave the venom deep.
There is no antidote,
Just time
Will make the difference...

I fell into your arms
Like tall grass.
You wave
And rock my soul,
Sing song and stay,
Persway,
As if I have no words to say…

To look deep into your eyes,
Should I say yes
To your love?

I sink in your arms,
Shimmering grass…

June 2024

~ 64 ~

ICE BREAKER

I boomeranged your thoughts,
Looked in your soul for more
But couldn't find.
Because your deepest secrets stay intact,
They keep the silence and resilience to love.

March 2023

~ 65 ~

MY FANTASY

Flow relentlessly, spinning around
Your fantasy.
You are my tournesol,
That spins my soul around.
You are the golden heart of earth
And soft shadow of the moon.
I try to carry gently
Veil of your wind
And to protect the fragile dust around.
You failed me and rushed,
I spilled the holy grail.

August 2023

~ 66 ~

TOUCH BASE

Touch base
With no emotion,
As if your heart has never touched my soul,
As if your lips have never kissed me,
Just touch base
With low notes,
With voice texting,
Or just emoji nod.
You know the rules with exes -
Just touch base,
Revoke the right to love
Once you've left.

August 2023

~ 67 ~

COMFORT ZONE

You told me to forget the comfort zone
And break the promise to myself.
About the tranquility of the mind,
To step up in the game.

To break the rules of games,
To level up.
I lost my sleep
And found strength somewhere
To be myself
In the enduring chaos game.

And suddenly
Felt a comfort zone again.
Tranquility of soul
A clear mind.

Sometimes
When pushing towards the goal
You have to slow down
For a moment,

Discover a pace
That wins the race
For you,
For staying true.

July 2023

~ 68 ~

WINDY

Wind song whispers me lullaby,
Lush greenery moves in a strange dance.
You would have used to the rhythms of night,
But every moment brings a new melody.
Why move with wind,
Why catch its ecstatic joyful flow?
No reason, just for love of wind,
Soaking in the air bath,
Arms wide open...

August 2023

~ 69 ~

KISS

How many kisses did you make real,
Sweet, brisk, long-lasting,
Passionate, desperate, sudden, unresponsive,
Unforgettable, first, last, bitter, French, light,
Faded, smudged, indifferent, automatic, usual,
TV-induced,
And,
Just like that.

August 2023

~ 70 ~

NODES OF LOVE

Tie the node so no escape.
No wave can break,
No air can erode with time.
The node that is mathematically impossible
And time resistant,
That will turn into a solid rock.
But then eventually you say
Rocks turn to dust.
Without us,
Without light that we emit.
So, tie the node,
Invisible,
Unreal.

September 2023

~ 71 ~

RAIN

We took a rain for granted once again,
And it was night that fell behind the curtain.
You took my hand with yours that trembled
And kissed my fingers one after another.
I promised things, that never had a chance,
Appear and prolong existing.
Your trembling hands were always there for me,
And kisses that you left on my cheeks and fingers.
Although the rain was washing all the traces.

July 2023

~ 72 ~

TURBAN OF LOVE

I never dreamed
To be caught in a moment,
To be taken away with an air balloon,
To be blown away
By the sparkle and dazzle,
In a crimson light
Of a rose's smile,
And the dew on your cheeks
And the sounds of stars.

July 2023

~ 73 ~

PAPER BIRDS

I want to hold a sting of paper birds
And breathe the wind.
I want to kiss your lips and whisper songs
And splash the puddles stamping feet.
My paper birds will fly and catch on fire
The ash will fall into your hands.
The string will hold on to the air
Because your lips have told me a lie.

May 2010

~ 74 ~

FREEZE

I freeze without you
And my soul is thirsty dry.
And silence overwhelming
When I am without you.

I don't hear the night
Without you.
As in the past
I lost the path to the valley.

As roads and passages
Are washed off the earth.
And even the island,
Where refuge is common,
Has disappeared
Without a trace.

I freeze without you
And try to warm up
Under the stars
That fire up at night.

As if I was not existing,
Not present in the reality of the earth.

August 2023

~ 75 ~

COLOURS OF LOVE

Wind sweeping across the sea,
Breaking the waves,
Pushing the whites,
Pushing the blues,
Smearing the colours in me.
Sometimes we fall
And go back.
We dream, we scream,
We fight, feel no regret.
But light will heal
With colour spill,
With waves that split,
With wind that blows.
The leaves that shimmer crystal bright
And waterfall
In the morning light.

June 2023

~ 76 ~

LOVE

I give you snow,
Crystal books
Made of airy snowflakes
That dance in sky.

I give you fields
And my footprints in grass,
Morning dew on my feet.

Will give you this salt
Soft and fluffy
From sea,

Where poems were born,
Where doubts arise,
Beading intricate patterns,

Snow-white waves
In the deep blue sea.
Don't hide it from me.

Sorrow days in the dark clouds,

Where the sound of my soul echoes
Multiple facets.
Let it sing,
Let it be...

October 2023

~ 77 ~

BECOMING A WORD LOVE

I want to become a word
That touches your lips,
That breaks the air,
Becoming a sound.
So powerful,
So free.
A wave of sounds,
A chaotic movement, -
So disturbing
Worth listening to.
How do I become a word
As promised?
To change the world,
Confess to love,
Save lives,
Sign songs...

September 2023

~ 78 ~

POSTCARD

Old-fashioned.
Call me old-fashioned.
Call me romantic,
Absurd,
Neurotic,
Naive.
Call me blonde,
Call me nicknames.
That won't change
My love note
Dropped in the stream of mail
On a paper, hand-drawn postcard.

September 2023

~ 79 ~

BREATHTAKING

We walk in the moonlight,
Keeping traces invisible on the sand.
We swim in the ocean
Of night, where waters have no end,
Where waters touch the horizon
On the invisible line,
Where we draw together
Some scribbles
In unknown signs.
We told each other stories
About the giant whale
Who agreed to take us
Together to the edge of time.
I see you as a fairytale,
Invisible moon dust at night.

August 2023

~ 80 ~

AME

I don't know how to pronounce your name,
Sweet name,
Fast and swish sound,
Like a guitar...
Haunting sound of strings
Of your soul guitar.
And I remember you,
Standing by the river,
Over the sunset, bending,
Like a big protector
Of dancing shadows,
Some fantastic creatures,
Not known yet to you and me.
May be these creatures
Are just imagination,
Or fruits of being vulnerable
And scared.
I feel just right with you,
Although I cannot connect the letters
Of your mysterious name.
Tomorrow you may be gone.
With sound of music

Of your guitar,
Like a silver ringing string,
I said, just like a string.
Maybe I'll catch your name then...
Like a tumbleweed,
You roll away with no trace.
Just the sound of your guitar
Stays echoing deep in my memory.

May 2023

~ 81 ~

A TRAP

Time has a trap
For a moment like this.
To stay forever
In a black hole
That has no time
Or space.
It creates an opportunity
For memories to stay,
Within,
Without escape.
I float with you just above the surface
Without superficial and pretentious thoughts,
Without interfering emotions,
As moment froze in one kiss.
I float with you as time unfolds
In something understandable yet vague.
Your arms touch droplets of my tears
And draw a smile on my face.

April 2023

EMOJI

Picture this, in one sound or word,
Capturing waves of human thought.
You send me emoji instead,
Which does make it count
I guess as a sound,
As a modern like hieroglyph.
Umbrella for rainy emotions
That flood us
Invisible
On the other end of the line.
Old fashioned method of writing
Making it to modern world
In a childish way.

April 2023

~ 83 ~

THE TYPO

One letter flew away
Like a bird,
Out of cage of structured sense,
It made a sound
Called misunderstanding.
They called it a typo.
A mistake,
Produced by a human
Being inattentive.
But it can trigger
Wired things in life,
One letter misinterpreted
And left behind...
Why we invented
Such complicated way
To give our thoughts
Material existence?

June 2023

~ 84 ~

DELICATE MOMENT

You caught me today
In a delicate moment
Of making decisions
That wiped out years of trust.

The moment when paper reveals
The invisible ink of one's true self.
You write your confessions
Somewhere in closet
The one full of skeletons
Ready to fight.

Decisions are walking on bridge
Are suspended
Between two identical
Mountains of gold.

So, you might feel suspended in air
For a moment,
Like a butterfly, free
Of responsible dust.

But a moment like this
Won't last, they detain
The brave,
Caught in a moment.

Making a decision,
Surender at last.

December 2023

~ 85 ~

JENGA GAME

I knocked down the Jenga of your arguments
With one kick
Called the truth.
Rolled back,
Behind a curtain,
Step down,
Still not happy with defeat,
Your arguments one by one
Are out together in another Jenga.
With someone else.
Still thirsty for the game.
I dried my efforts
Winning by confronting.
You play a game not fair,
Sneaky little game.
So, checkmate darling.
Jinx your Jenga.

August 2023

~ 86 ~

CHANCE

I gave you a chance
And called it love,
Don't let it go.
No matter how hard it hurts,
No matter how shaken the ground is,
No matter how much it rains.
You have a chance
And that my friend is key
To all the doors that you can find,
Unless you turn away from me
And there are no locks to be found.

June 2023

~ 87 ~

IT ALL BEGINS

It all begins with love,
You said.
My tears will be seen
By all my friends.
Not because of a love story,
Not because of confessions
You made with such passion.
It all begins with love
A path, a laughter, happiness.
But where does this road end?
Grass dries, and dust turns greyish
With howling desert putting spell,
Attracting us.
Inertia of lies, swear words, sarcasm
Will put an end to love
If weak and scribbled
And not a masterpiece.

May 2023

~ 88 ~

SEA OF LOVE

Surviving the sea of love.
Climbing quickly the steep steps,
Bringing forgotten keys
Hiding and finding again.

Calling in void,
Catching simmering sound,
Recoding reverb.
Playing day and night
The music of love.

Surviving the five-feet wave
That crashes your feelings,
That crashes your voice
In a deep hidden place
Greetings for love.

The whisper at first
Thirsty for love,
A ringing tone,
Chorus that sings in the clouds
You hear it all.

Chocolate-flavoured,
Vanilla, tobacco,
Strawberry, cherry,
Or just sweet honey drops,
Lips whisper sounds of love.

August 2023

~ 89 ~

THIEVES OF LOVE

Passing through the city,
Full speed ahead.
Running from thieves of love.
Don't look back,
Feeling rushed,
Overwhelming by waves
Up and down,
Up and down.
Hit
The nose of the ship,
Hit my heart
With wave of love,
With way of being there
In a heat of love,
In a heart of passion.
Running from the thieves of love,
Running ahead of yourself.
Running,
Feeling the wave
Of unexpected.
Fusion of love and rage.
Heart drop,

Heartbeat,
Heart sink,
Heart break.
Hiding from thieves of love.
Finding a quiet cave.
Breaking the waves of rage.
Singing to sunshine rays.
Bringing the best of self.
Finding the strength for truth.
Don't be close to these,
Who look at your love
As a thing.
They use it,
Lose it.

September 2023

~ 90 ~

IT WAS

It was a flirtation,
Some twisting hair,
Some steering
Of emotions wheel.
And some misspoken words,
Thrown in the air
Like raindrops.
Misunderstanding,
Apologetic moves,
Retreat,
Abandoned feelings.
And then
There was some love,
That grew like ocean,
And spoke to me
In the unknown words.
About worlds
To be created,
Not conquered.
The words
That weaved
The canvas or a novel

The story,
All about you and me.

September 2023

~ 91 ~

SO

I saw the petals dancing at your feet
With every step.
And the wind was whispering the rhythms
With every breath you take.
I saw you dancing with the stars,
At sunrise, when the moon is still there.
I saw you signing with the wind
As if you don't care.
But then you gathered petals in your hands
And jumped with them like a toddler
Up and down.
I saw your inner child dance
And laugh, and cry, and smile.
Some say it is a dream
To see your inner child free.
Some dreams should stay just dreams, -
I say, for then they are sweeter.

August 2023

~ 92 ~

LOVE WORD

A word escaped my thoughts,
It interfered with the air,
It took its time.
It broke the pattern of the smoke,
Travelled several miles,
Came back to me,
It missed my thoughts.
But I have sent the word away again
To leave more traces in the air,
To touch the souls.
To be a free word bird.

March 2024

~ 93 ~

L'AMOUR

Tower of the thousand rocks
You built patiently these years.
You found shapes that filled the need,
Round shapes smooth to touch.
There were no gaps, just smooth surface,
Holding one another
With patience and persistence.
You finished tower-shaped
like a question mark,
Like doubt.
It fell with sound echoing in ocean
Deep motion resonated in a seaweed,
Creating waves that came to shore,
And moved the rocks again
So, you can build them.

August 2023

~ 94 ~

COLOURS OF LOVE

When love
Is blurring colours
And making grey day,
Go away,
You take a brush
And with one emotion
Draw a line to do the same
And fail.
As love does this
In a remarkable way…

June 2023

~ 95 ~

SOUND

I love to listen to
To the droplets of your sounds
Falling on a keyboard of your piano,
Breaking silence
In thousand pieces,
Resembling tiny crystal Venus
Dancing witchy dance
In early sunrise...
But now no sun
Can light the darkness
Of this hush tranquility
Interrupted by the sound of broken piano,
Crying these droplets
In vast space...

December 2023

~ 96 ~

HIDDEN FEELINGS

Somehow, we play our real feelings
Pretending they don't exist,
In quantum state of their hanging
Like falling plates behind closed doors.
We won't know if they brake or not
Until we open those doors
And witness
The pieces of the falling plates,
As real as it gets.
Same for my anger, shame, joy, fear.
Until acknowledgment they stay
In my mind, that is quiet and peaceful.
They stay tight until you say
First word material and real.

December 2023

~ 97 ~

I WONDER

I never held you hand
I never kissed your lips
We met just once
And I
Lost all my sleep to the debt of love.
I never dreamed of you
You just appeared like this
In fog of winter ice
On the thin edge of the lake.
I wonder if one day
A simple gesture trick
Will tell you that I am
In total debt to you.

May 2023

~ 98 ~

TWO HEARTBEATS

They say everything will start with love
I read you heartbeat close to mine
But mine is warmer and abrupt.
They say you won't survive the passion
Of aging measurable life
That molds your heart.
Wild lichen spreads its tentacles around
Connections of the former friends
Who keeps their silence.
And friends will tell
Love is just a word without spell
That was inverted to prevent
Destruction of the alliance.
Yet their heart is not so close to mine,
Not selfish, just preoccupied
With ego's passion.
So, it takes two hearts to keep the rhythm,
Shake time, break lichen.
Their rhythm is smashing...

May 2023

~ 99 ~

IT RAINED

It rained the words on me again,
Some dude mixed up topography in motion
And felt like ordinary rain,
But cold is indifferent for emotions.
You love for letters fetish-like
Amuse my eyes, but not the ears.
I listen to your silly words
About love, about tears.
It rains like words, but senseless
Pointless.
No worries, my umbrella is tough.

September 2023

~ 100 ~

CHILDISH

I closed my eyes
And felt like a child again,
Rolled up, blanket up,
Far away from the adult world.
In a pink castle,
With a teddy bear,
In a cardboard car,
In a rocking chair.
I closed my eyes,
Saw fantastic beasts,
Ogres and elves,
Fairies on dragons.
Faraway,
From where I am,
In a bookshelf,
In a keepsake.

September 2023

~ 101 ~

CHORUS OF LETTERS

You are conducting
Chorus of the falling letters
That fall into the river of the words,
That flows in the ocean of the books.
You are the writer, seeker of the wisdom,
You are a magician turning words into gold.

September 2023

HORIZON

He told me in my sleep
"My favourite place, a horizon,
Where sea meets the sky",
And ever-changing colours
Define space along the line.

Where night will dip its darkness
In milky waters of the clouds.
And pink flamingo morning
Would
Swipe the greys.

And where dusty sunshine
Of hot summer days
Will be cooled down
By blue moon dust.

And winter ice fog
Breaks the lines
In deep blues of sunny ice.

Where rain will dance as bubbles

Weaving tiny dancers in the sky
Breaking the transparent lines
With vibrations of the light.

August 2023

~ 103 ~

MY PACE

I don't live in someone else's dream,
Dance to the tune that someone else is whistling.
You take my hand no matter what,
I let you hop with me along.
I made atonement with the world.
Not yet acknowledged just imagined.
As a scandalous art piece,
Installation,
Acupuncture piece,
Staring at the world.

August 2023

~ 104 ~

BEFORE MYSELF

I have been here before, in other life;
I felt the sun rays run through my veins,
Pushing blood to sky,
When I ran up the hill to you.
I rescued you from thieves of love,
From silent battles of temptations,
Of desperate self-sabotage and greed.
I still remember sails of the town
Reflecting heat and deepening the shades.
You are in the past they told me
Or the future, not nowadays.
Not here, so they say.
I have been here before,
Stepped on the platform
To speak the words of truth
And sing the song.
The sound is still there in the ocean,
It echoed quietly as we moved on.
No journey can be taken just for granted,
Without adventure, risks, surprise.
Take just a trip through life,
Observing motion?

Or choose a steeper path.
There is no honey in success, remember.
There are just bees
With a noble honest quest.
I have been here before
And walked the paths.
Those thousand years
Flatten rocks to dust.
We all have been here before,
Just some of us cannot remember.

August 2023

4

CITIES

CITY LIGHTS

Just before night
Covers the buildings
City lights glow,
With traffic flow
They make lines,
Continuous streaks.
I love to stay
In the backseat
And watch those lights,
Harness them,
As untamed glowing horses,
With a fire-like mane.
Just before night like
Creature
Crawls under the bed,
The city lights dim,
And stars blink
In a delicate rhythm.
I cannot harness the stars
As the moon or the sun,
I could only draw them
With water and color

With charcoal and pen
On the snow that melts
Once morning.

August 2020

~ 106 ~

ABANDONED CITIES

Abandoned cities dream of better days,
When ash did not fall from the sky,
When colours mixed with purple not the grey,
And rain was not there to cry.
We see them gloomy, dreamy, dark.
Sharp edges make them medieval,
Looking with their hollow eyes
In the souls of trembling human beings.
Abandoned cities dream of better days...

April 2024

~ 107 ~

DOORS OPENED

Just a pick in this door—
Someone left a small space,
Just to have a small glance,
Chat with someone about
Things we see behind doors.
Imagine life we never knew
As being part of it
With doors wide open,
As if the spaces between ones on the other side
Are small and close.
And no divisions,
No walls between the lives that coexisted
In small opening of door that squinted,
That asked to stay closed
Tight and dark.
Yet they all peak
With their imagination
And rumors spreading word around
About curtains, slippers, bathrobes,
About Uber meal on stairs
Parcels at the doors,
Unopened mail shuttered on the floor.

And doors move slowly
With the wind
Inviting rumors as we speak.

October 2023

~ 108 ~

VINTAGE ALLURE

On of the boxes on river Sienna
The lock broke, and books fell into the water.
I saw a girl crying as vintage dissolved in the River
Colorless pages
Slowly floating apart.
I look at her flowers, pale and lifeless
Blue tiny flowers on pink riverbed.
Framed into a beige wooden wrecker
An old Chinese porcelain doll waving back.

June 2023

~ 109 ~

A SCENE FROM PARIS

She looked at him
Through the stained glass
Of Notre Dame,
Trying to tell him
All about love.
Her voice was on fire,
Her tears dried out.
Her face was coloured
With colours of saints.
She made a confession,
He knew it already.
I scar people deeply
With emotional pain.
He looked at her lips
Of saint-coloured pallets,
And told her to lie.
Stop fire emotions,
Stop being dramatic,
Stop being pollution
Of love.
Her voice stopped abruptly,
She shadowed briefly

As if someone put
A cover on her.
A motionless shadow
Being dramatic
Behind a glass
Of cathedral at night.
He looked at her lips
No words, No tears.
No beauty, no light.
I bear you darling,
Your truth and emotions,
Your fire, your scars,
Pain, challenge,
Just live.
She looked at him scared,
And tears broken down,
The church was on fire,
Because of this sin.

August 2023

~ 110 ~

DREAM CITY

I had a dream of a city -
Empty, dusty, cleared from trees.
I was riding a ghost horse
In a desert city,
That I knew one day and loved.

I was chasing ghosts on a ghost horse.
Telling them memories and singing the songs.
But they didn't listen to me, scared and lost.
I had a dream of a ghost horse
In a dusty city with stars on gilded roofs.

There was one man in a square
Waiting for me and waving.
As if he knew I was there.
A dream has ended then,
I never knew who he was.

I was riding a ghost horse
In a desert city.
Still hear the wind blowing,
Whistling the song.

Ghost horse in a desert city
Ghost town I loved.

August 2023

5

MIND

~ 111 ~

PULLING STRINGS

Attached to the strings of desires,
Like tamed by someone else's dreams,
Dependent on saliva of the ads,
Spitting on the screens,
Shouting at you
With sounds of fatal attractions.
Would you mind
Breaking free?
Pulling the strings
Of the tension
That detaches your mind?
Would you feel free
After all?

April 2023

~ 112 ~

FACT FULL

Drenched in facts,
Feeling like a toad near a newsstand.
Fact of full
Till my stomach hurts.
Till the nauseous subconscious
Spills the endless emotions.
But no action,
No reaction,
That brings change.
How far would you go
To devour
Facts,
Mind completely blown,
But helpless
Of my own indifference,
Unable to act,
Unable to judge.
Fact fools are
Full of facts.

April 2023

~ 113 ~

JUNGLE SOUL

Hey Jungle soul,
Look inside
This jungle soul,
Find a fire burning,
Jungle soul.
Tell me right—
How do you cope,
The world is on fire,
Drying tears...
Jungle soul
Whisper "witches"...
See the water
Calming fears,
See the waves,
Rocking chairs,
Jungle soul
Signing, whistling...

March 2024

~ 114 ~

LECTURE

Be in the woods
Away from the hustle.
Defend your mind
From news wars,
From a loop of news,
That bring to knees
The common sense
In judgement.
Why everything
Is so damn opinionated,
So, chewed
for easy swallowing
By rigid, weak and lazy minds?
Just press the Jukebox of a chat
And bot will tell you
How to love,
How to impress the boss
With knowledge.
And never bothered
If it's fake or true.
News fly
No matter what,

And wash away
The truth,
That dare to clinch
And hold
To last handwritten note.

January 2024

OBSESSION

The mediocrity has left the building.
I am waiting for its next move...
It leaches on the thirst for news,
For entertainment, for bursts of sensation.
For a short description, headlines, leads,
The concentrated broth.
"L'écume du jour" we call it,
Creme de la creme.
But, in fact, it is a moment we'll forget
Most likely in the wake of the next uproar.

April 2023

~ 116 ~

STRANGER

Hey stranger,
Born in a country
That never existed,
Not now, not beyond.

Forgive the sorrow
That runs your life,
Depressive refuge
That you called home.

Forgive my pain
For others,
Who lived in a city
That existed not.

Don't pity those,
Their choice, and sigh,
For anger, fears,
Love, betrayals, loss,

For rain of tears,
Taste of salty grief,

Your tears, mine,
Theirs,
It doesn't matter.

August 2010

~ 117 ~

MANKIND SHIP

I feel like in the middle of the ocean,
The roundabout for ships around me.
The center of the centrifuge,
That turns around emotions
And stirs the memories of humankind.

January 2024

~ 118 ~

PRELUDE

For those who gave up.
They are the inspiration
For those who do not want
And never will give up.

The failure created
The Opposite direction
Of a never-ending quest.

To seek the change
In the blowing snow,
To climb the rocks,
To tame the waves.

To challenge self
Not others.
To stay yourself,
Discover the truth.

To speak the truth
When facing lies and cowards.
To step on burning rocks

To stay still
When the winds are high.
And to return back home
When time comes.

February 2022

FOUNDATION OF FREE SPEECH

Flattened ground, gathered dust,
Washed feet, spoken words,
Clapping hands, shuttered dreams,
Broken bones, closed eyes.

Spoken once, broken verse,
Shouting crowd, firewalls,
Drums and spears, cry and tears,
Flattened ground, raising rock.

No reason speaking truly,
If the rock is left to dust,
If the ground is flattened round,
No rock, no past, no dust.

No platform for the speaker,
If the freedom is left to die
In the past we did not own.
No voice, no truth or lie.

Kneel to clean the rock from dust,
Keep it raising, so the truth

Steps on rocks and not the crowd,
One step further, not above.

*Remembering the rock of the speaker on Ancient Agora,
that inspired me in summer.*

August 2023

~ 120 ~

THERE IS A LAND

There is a land that I call home.
Where sun goes up and down every day,
Where rain river washes off my grief
And rounds up my life rock on a lakeshore.

I speak no sign, no words, no music there.
I colour the air with the smoky days.
The land of stone walls and golden beer.
The land of smoky wood and wild grass.

I dip my fingers in the maple syrup
And eat the snow in an innovative way.
And every lake reflects the eyes of stars.
They shine crisper on this side on earth.

Or so we thought about crisp reflections,
Sometimes, they blur with movement, rain and Fog.
We keep this silence for the decade straight
And then we burst into a fountain of emotions.

We take a no as the shortest answer,
Bring up the argument as long as the Milky Way.

About so many ways to paint the snow,
In a poetic way, so to say.

It's a polite way of a truth seeker,
To paint words in multicoloured scheme.
To choose the colours of the different corners,
From parts of Earth that never be the same.

September 2023

~ 121 ~

LIKE HOME

This place once felt like home,
Once was a refuge for emotions,
Now just a sofa and a bed,
With cozy chair and a table.

A glass that separates a world,
Your face behind it,
Touch of breath and drops of dew
That left a nostalgic trace
On the window to the other worlds.

But still this place is no home,
But a station.
A still-life of another page
Of ever-changing life,
The race, the action.
But it feels like home, nevertheless.

June 2023

TIME

Time as a sculptor,
Waves as a brush,
Salt as turpentine,
Algae as paint.
Shifting earth,
Wrinkling rock,
Fighting with time,
Adjusting the clock.

August 2023

~ 123 ~

TO SUMMER 1989

A thousand stitches in my heart
Will tell the story.
About the embroidered pain, regret,
About joy and sorrow.
About love that kept us all together,
About thousand-mile journey of the past,
About letters read by heart but not the eyes,
About being true to who you are.
All being there in one concerto beat.
My heart stitches came undone one day,
As loose threads kept holding on emotions.
I use them now to mend the other people's Grief…

January 2024

~ 124 ~

OPPORTUNITY

I missed that moment.
Hands in the air,
Catching dust
And waving with the wind.
I missed that moment...
Sound of it still ringing
The happiness of light
And ever-lasting hope.
The particles of moment
Are still there,
I see them
In the smile on your face,
In the hint of laughter,
In your steps on the sidewalk—
Fast-paced steps.
We are forever in a hurry
And miss the moments
That stand still.

June 2023

~ 125 ~

THERE WAS AN ANGEL

There was an angel
With a bleeding heart
That whispered in my ear.
A wired angel
Holding hand near the heart.
It called me love
And sang a song of glory
About those who do not have one.

June 2023

~ 126 ~

WHEN I HEAR THE SOUND OF WAR

Or maybe I cried in a way you have never seen me cry.
Or maybe it rained,
Or maybe you caught the wind
With breath of the dead.
Maybe you talked to the dead
When gathered leaves from a ground
In dark autumn day,
In dark human day.
Just when the sun was setting down
It evoked a dream,
To lighten the night,
To catch the rain
For fresh water
To water some flowers.

October 2023

~ 127 ~

DARK DAYS

There are no colder days,
There are dark days,
The ones you wish the sun
Won't notice on its orbit.
But here they are
With the strange grey dawn
With obscured grief
And the grim smile of storm.

July 2023

~ 129 ~

TREES ARE TURNING GREY

Birch trees are tuning aging grey
As winter won't let them
Turn their hair dusty green
Like spring previewed when mixing colours.
Wide eyes of the lake
Will darken their mood
Still looking into the sky,
Covered with clouds
That hide all the stars
That breath stardust on us
From deep purple darkness.
We also touch the spring,
But burn our fingers with cold
Just in the end of March,
Where cold is still in reign...

June 2023

~ 130 ~

TALK TO THE DEAD

It seems we won't allow dead
Keep silence any longer
Earth crust got thinner, shred,
Eroded by water,
That washed away
A balanced refuge, obstacles and rocks.
So, they awake, all surprised,
At dawn to sing their songs.
Their life is so short as we know,
Ephemeral for ghosts.
Their speech interrupted
With chaos of words.
Time for the dead is so different
From Earth-like.
They would hope the colours of soil
Could paint miracles over their bones
With eternal peace and tranquility.
Web them softly in dreamy fog,
Spray with lily tree scent
So sweet it will choke you.
There are also brooks
Of spring water that joyfully

Bring some laughter to ghost tirades.
Make them thrill and
Horror fused haunting.
But know they melt with spring,
Disappear.
They'll appear at night,
At the sunset with grace.
They will gather the dust
Dandelions left in a hurry.

February 2024

~ 131 ~

BE WATER, CHANGE

Be water, change,
Wash off the superficial.
In gazing sun
Blaze moves the wind.
I hold my breath
And touch the burning air.
Dig up the dirt
From my grandfather's grave.
And put it in my veins.
Wash off the blaze,
The greed, the sins.
Reborn from ashes
In a transparent form,
Born to re-bloom the earth again.

February 2022

~ 132 ~

DESERT-HEARTED

The desert in heart
Burns a ground around,
Makes a desert around,
Full of skeleton dust.
Blindfolded with power,
Narcissistic ambitions,
Medieval mindset
And rhetoric ambiance,
Cold hearted man
Brings the world
To the point,
Where droplets of hope
Are like rain on Mars.

August 2010

~ 133 ~

SMALL TALK TO EARTH

I am talking to subconscious of the earth
That spells the rivers flooding,
That whispers scary words to avalanches
And breaks the ice with anger and despair.
I know one thing that its subconscious
Will rise soon closer to the surface.
The earth will see the world naked,
Drawn in charcoal, colourless.

September 2010

IRIADA TALES

Poetry Collection
by Irene Smirnova

Copyright © 2024 by Irene Smirnova. All rights reserved.
No part of this book may be used or reproduced
without written permission of the author.
ISBN: 978-1-0689158-0-2

Collaborating editor: Aparna Kumar
Production manager: Alexis Smirnov
Illustrations and photos: Irene Smirnova
Publisher: Atelier Bloom Editions

 Irene Smirnova is a Canadian writer and an artist living in Montreal, Canada. She has Bachelor degree in journalism and literature, college degree in visual effects and animation. She worked over the past few decades as an art and film critic, and as a digital and visual artist.

Irene mostly known as an award winning visual effects artist, who contributed to over 60 Films and TV shows. Her oil paintings, digital artwork are exhibited over the past years in Canada and US.

Irene's poetry is inseparable from her art. Poetry sparks new ideas, new themes in artworks.

At the same time, her poems absorb artistic metaphors, use colourful landscapes as a background for emotional story.

www.ingramcontent.com/pod-product-compliance
Lightning Source LLC
Chambersburg PA
CBHW051546010526
44118CB00022B/2601